D1432600

ROME

ROME

POEMS

DOROTHEA LASKY

LIVERIGHT PUBLISHING CORPORATION

A DIVISION OF W. W. NORTON & COMPANY

NEW YORK   LONDON

For information about permission to reproduce selections from this
book, write to Permissions, Liveright Publishing Corporation,
a division of W. W. Norton & Company, Inc.,
500 Fifth Avenue, New York, NY 10110

For information about special discounts for bulk purchases,
please contact W. W. Norton Special Sales at
specialsales@wwnorton.com or 800-233-4830

Manufacturing by Courier Westford
Book design by Lovedog Studio
Production manager: Anna Oler

Library of Congress Cataloging-in-Publication Data

Lasky, Dorothea, 1978–
[Poems. Selections]
ROME : poems / Dorothea Lasky. — First edition.
pages cm
ISBN 978-0-87140-939-3 (hardcover)
I. Title.
PS3612.A858A6 2014
811'.6—dc23
2014025222

Liveright Publishing Corporation
500 Fifth Avenue, New York, N.Y. 10110
www.wwnorton.com

W. W. Norton & Company Ltd.
Castle House, 75/76 Wells Street, W1T sQT

1 2 3 4 5 6 7 8 9 0

CONTENTS

CONSUME MY HEART AWAY; SICK WITH DESIRE

AND FASTENED TO A DYING ANIMAL

—*William Butler Yeats, "Sailing to Byzantium"*

ROME

HUNTERS

Their bloodlust is what made them different from me

I saw the man with an albino moose
Holding his antlers with pride
In the photo
By your bedside

And all I could think of
Was how scared the dead moose must have been

Now when I try to eat an animal, I hear crying
Not laughter
Now when I try to sing,
I do not
Instead I walk along
And everyone on the earth is an enemy
I have no confidante, no squire

All of it is because
Of how badly you lied to me

I thought it was just you and me
Or at the very least a tiny epigram

Madness is eating animals
I am mad
But I don't kill anything
I sit there bloodless
And my lust, too
It rings

WHY POETRY CAN BE HARD FOR MOST PEOPLE

Because speaking to the dead is not something you want to do
When you have other things to do in your day
Like take out the trash or use the vacuum
In the edge between the stove and cupboard
Because the rat is everywhere
Crawling around
Or more so walking
And it doesn't even notice you
It has its own intentions
And is searching for that perfect bag of potato chips
    like you once were
Because life is no more important than eating
Or fucking
Or talking someone into fucking
Or talking someone into something
Or sleeping calmly and soundly
And all you can hope for are the people who put that calm in you
Or let you go into it with dignity
Because poetry reminds you
That there is no dignity
In living
You just muddle through and for what
Jack Jack you wrote to him
You wrote to all of us

I wasn't even born
You wrote to me
A ball of red and green shifting sparks
In my parents' eye
You wrote to me and I just listened
I listened I listened I tell you
And I came back
No
Poetry is hard for most people
Because of sound

NEVER DID AMOUNT TO ANYTHING

AFTER CATULLUS, #43

Hi there, dear sister, I'm sad
But here to tell you
That you never did amount to anything
Facial expressions just like your mother
Nose by no means tiny
Married a couple of people
So now you sit in a house
Cleaning or not cleaning a window
Newsflash: no one cares about time
But you do it like it's so moral being punctual
Truly an actress, but you poorly acted the part
Of someone who isn't crazy
No I can't say your ankles *are* fat
But dear lady, who would have had your ass
Except now I do
Seemingly connected we are, in the worst way
And so I must tell you
You are a no-good person
A criminal, really, a scoundrel
No, really, a liar
He said the person was cold, maybe a bit disdainful
I said, welcome to my life
You know some people like history

Or want to make history
But I am history
If you would have fucked me
I would have been ok being Plath
But instead I'm Sexton
If somebody asks me what I like
It's not food or sex
It's looking at things and being in love
Not sure what of this you did offer me
Never did amount to anything
So with this
I go

PORN

All types of porn are horrific
I just watched a woman fuck a hired hand
In her marble kitchen while her friends looked on
The title of the movie was *Divorce Party*
And throughout his big cock, her skinny thighs
Her friends shouted, nah girl, now you're free

But no she's not she's in a movie
And now I am crying
Because the man looks like an ex-boyfriend
Or my half brother
My boss
A monster
Someone who left me in the dark
Someone who darkened me
A million times over

I've only fucked seven guys in my whole life
But I've watched more porn than you ever will
Hours and hours
A woman and a dog
Three women
A hairy fruit
Four bending over backwards

Vomit sex
The underplay
Of tendril
In motion

I watch porn
Cause I'll never be in love
Except with you dear reader
Who thinks I surrender
But who's to say this stanza is not porn
Calculated and hurtful
All my friends say I'm free
And yes, maybe I am
But are you free
No, you'll never be
I've got you in my grasp
I've got you right here in my room
Once again

WHAT'S WORSE

What's worse—a cheap man or a cad
What's worse—a man who eats the fingers or one who does not
What's worse—doggy style or up the ass
No, what's worse—his face or the face of the individual
I mean, what's worse—knowing you or knowing later
Knowing nothing
Oh Alligator
I just want the eyes
Up to my eyes
What's worse
To never have them
To have them only in part
What's worse
To be endlessly waiting
To be endlessly waiting
What's worse—nothing or nothing
What's worse
What's worse than nothing
What's worse
No, what's worse

WINTER

There was a lonely summer

Where I took the string and unraveled the magic circle from
  everything

It was because of you, and what you did to me

No it was winter

When I drank cola right by his head

The girl said her poem was called Winter

The boy said his name was The Sea

If I could have wrapped you in purple robes

For the rest of my life

I would have

If I could have gone to the sea, I would have

But oh, what it was you did to me

Instead they wrap me in gold cloth

Carry me into the center of everything

The magic circle I had in my hand

They unwrapped me until I multiplied

They took the red string which bound me to you

They sank it in the center of the ocean

I AM EDDIE MURPHY

Girl, I heard that you got a place
Where you tell jokes, à la Eddie Murphy, 1985
But how do you do that
I am Eddie Murphy
I heard
That you do wine tastings with Eddie Murphy
In the vineyards of Italia
And I am confused
I am not there
I am Eddie Murphy
I am snorting cocaine off of tanned Italian backsides
While ten young men
Suck my gigantic dick
For two hundred hours
Do you eat a fine steak dinner with Eddie Murphy
But I am still hungry
And it is 4 am on the West side
I am going home to my majestic marble linoleum
I tell the jokes here
And if you want to
Come into my house
Introduce yourself first
Don't just go walking in
And telling the people you know them

Or you are the one they have been waiting for

They aren't waiting for anything

I make royalties on my sort of thing

I give them what they need

We are brethren

We are together

This is not about you

You write a punchline

Go up in front of the crowd

Say, I am the thing that makes you turn

But honey

It is a lie when you do it

You are the person outside the house

I am the one

Gracious enough

To let you in

PEOPLE DO REALLY BAD THINGS

People do really bad things
But I don't pay attention to most of them
I knew that Alex was my real friend
When he told me that one night
That true love cannot be calculated or contained
Despite the orb of blue fire
I always hold right up to my lips
It is hot and earthy
And full of red and green stars
But the one I love is not a plant to grow you in
The one I love goes driving thru the streets
My true friends have always been poets
Laura, and Eric
And the other people
The endless need of people crushing everything too, the sublime
Most of the time I am not the coral
Most of the time I am ashamed of my happiness
But that's because most of the time I do it in private
But not when my true love comes around
Then I do it everywhere
There is no place I would not be willing to make my true love sing
Even on the mountain where the seaweed is upturned into
    the heavens
Even then I would take his gentle hand with me anywhere

Even then I would not forsake anything he's done
Even if he did really bad things
I'd dive into the rich waters to help him

HORACE, TO THE ROMANS

I walk alone is what came into my head when I was sleeping
So I wrote you to get the water from which I was so thirsty
Poems are a puzzle
But animals are a beast is
So life is
Quiet life

Am I going to die and all I will have are these fucking poems
It doesn't get more real than this
Said the poet
Oh but you hate poems about poetry
And that's fine
Cause I am never going to send you my condolences when I kill it

To the lions I throw you
No, I must restore the broken-down altars that gave me so
    much sustenance
Those fallen busts and statues
That the idiots mention is missing a nose or a penis
When the statues are stone anyway
And I am living earth and bone

Ten times now, you crushed me
To tiny pieces then to dust

I just barely escaped the last time
And had to use my mind to coagulate the broken
Into mud then blood then semen
Formidable now, because of this evil mind

Which I used so many times under a lemon tree
Just dying to touch you
Because my love I love you
And will say it again and again to the air
Only the gods know how things end
Or whether the seas turn red in the end

What is there left unruined after all has been said
What will you make of me, ruined and soiled
My dead figure in a heap with the others
To distinguish, only in the dance
Still, look, look, look out for me
Our fathers taught us more than country

My father my father taught me more than dread
And your father taught you beast instead
So to the lions I throw you
That your arm and neck I so did covet
Will find your space here
Dead and dead and dead and dead

THE ORANGE FLOWER

What is between us
Is an orange flower

And it is blooming and blooming
And I can't I won't stop it

Still the sour flower of my vagina
Ruins everything

Blooming blooming
It changes the room

And I become almost
But not quite, the hummingbird

And I become almost, but not quite
The green birds that are missing

DEPRESSION

Depression—it's a public feeling
But what if I don't like anything as much as I pretend to

Darling Darling Darling
What if I don't even like you

The blue night with trees
Everything told me to feel something

And yet everything you said was a lie
And all my emotions were for nothing

Oh all they want you to do is cry cry cry
Cry they say Cry

The animal takes the shape of the spirit
And the I is no I

Hardly on the girl
But why?

I had two main ideas
That I brought to the forefront

But the ideas never moved the audience
To laughter, to pick the pockets

So I tapped a little peacock
With the fiery tail

Until no one knew what was there

Sadness
It's a public feeling

So I cry and cry
And the silver moon goes shining

Thunder and lightning
Thunder and lightning

I woke up in midmorning

And it was all chatter
Just thunder and lightning

DIET MOUNTAIN DEW

Something that I have
Thought of recently
Was my Diet Mountain Dew
Bottle in the kitchen refrigerator
I would like to be
Home
I would like to go
Home and to the places
Where people like me
It is really hard to
Keep the output
At an input
I go
And no one gives
A shit
All they want
Is the gift
Without even knowing
All the Diet Mountain Dew
That went into it
I go and people
Just listlessly want
Others to do it
For them

I ain't doing
Nothing anymore
For no one
Yeah that's right
I am going to show
This world
Exactly what it gave me
Which is strawberries
Which are the lilacs
Blooming round
The courtyard
Of the building
Where I catch my car
To go
I wear
A yellow dress

YOU WERE SO BLOND

I knew it I knew it
But you were so blond and soft
I forgot about all of the things I had to do
I needed to do
Like Sor Juana and Hannah Weiner
Your skin was so soft and young
I forgot about having a baby
Or painting my nails with eggcream
I went down to your place and thought about you in your thoughts
Your thoughts are not plain
But will anyone ever know them
Could anyone be more plainspoken than you
For a million emotions
Oh your emotions are a million colors
And it will take you a hundred years to find me again
Fuck, you fuck
I tried to make it easier on you this time
Instead I waited and waited
And never gave up
You know it's true what they say
Poetry is a destructive force
Your back in the photo
That she took
That is the thing I will always remember

I JUST HOPE I CAN SLEEP

I hope I can sleep and forget your name
I just hope that we drift apart
I hope that you stop writing me, like before
I hope that you discount the things I believe in
I hope that you don't even consider them
I hope that the rainbows go back and forth
And you don't stop them for me
And that I am in the midst of the tangled rainbow
And you aren't even thinking of me
I hope that when the land completely lit by rainbows
Is my new home you forget to ask me for my address
I hope that when the light shines on me
I don't look like anything or anyone
You think that you know
I hope that when you spot me in a field of honey
You keep on walking, walking past the honey
And drown yourself in a body of water
No I hope that there is a body of water
Which makes sense to you
An ocean of your own making

THE ROMAN POETS

The Roman poets brought me to this day
To see this thru

They marked me when I was little
They put the words in me

To be here
All the poems I've lost as papers I threw in the street

If I did it all to be here with you
If I took it all in

To sing it to you

Then yes love it was worth it
Just to live this life with you as my friend

And not a lover
But who cares anyway

The light was dim and drab
When I woke up and left it

In the light of the dawn
When I left this glorious animal body

To be the weather
That empties on the purple lawns

The end of things

THE OPEN SOUND OF FRENCH

Even the sound of French is open
And the children find me very interesting to look at
It is as if I am a TV show or supper
All my pretty babies who paint the winter chests
With red and gold and green

It was on the afternoon
In the small wooden town
That I was so mired in my act of jealousy
I did not pay attention
To the beauty of the dark church in front of me

And now you ask me
To meet you in a park after dark
Well it is too late too late
I am already flying

THE AMETHYST

All my life
It was a lie
To try to go towards bliss
But death is the ultimate blissfulness
To be a candy or a corpse
The world holds you on its tongue
And no one can save you
Not even your own children or your friends
So have a seat with the home of the dead
They will eat your colors
Until you are blank
The best thing to happen to you
The greatest happiness
To be an animal who is smoke
And beyond the mouth
That tears your bones from one another
To be a mound of meat
At the table of the living

BLAZING STAR LODGE

In the deepest part
I still loved him
Had gone with him
To the blazing star lodge

The place where
He had worn his brown suit
And blue tie
And had called his sister to tell her so

To match him, I wore my brown dress
And blue eyes
And painted a room inside the lodge
His favorite shade of green

The meal was simple
A bowl of lettuce
I cut the beets to his liking
I put the snails upon the plates

We talked and looked
At the things
We could submerge
In the immobile water

I did not commit this so as to tell you so
I did it because I was angry
And could not pick up the shells
Like I had wanted to for all those years

And he had promised
A place to stay
For at least a weekend
And said he would be there

And he was there
He always was
What a man in brown suit
The neatest purple script

In letters and notes
Coming all the way from the coastline
Even on my birthday
Had packed tiny jackalopes into an orange box and sent it

When I said for many weeks
That I was swamped with work
I meant I could not
Stop thinking about him

And in the night
Had put
Faces over other faces
To make me forget

Even through living
He taunted me with his arms
I saw them in pictures
Hold a thousand girls

And even I
Went to the edge
To see
What I could find

But nothing
Nothing
Ever else could quench
This desire for him

Nothing ever was close
To his face
So placid
By the ocean

I REMEMBER IN THE MORNING

I remember the morning when you left me
I remember it was midday when we left
I remember only the driving
All along in the half-dark and your face
In the orange shadows your grandfather made
And me in the mirror in the front room of the hospital
With the faded houndstooth on the chair where I sat
Where I called my friend
Who said to me that I was a wreath
And who to know what it was I did
I never believed him but I should have
You were so brutal
You were never wet
Now you come to my street in the sunrise and hold me
There are things you want to say but don't
There are things I want to say but I already said them
A year ago or two or five, when we first met
There were times I thought you knew I loved you
You never knew
We never were
I died
You died
That's it

JULY

In July, I put my face to the window
In June it had been a white line edged in blue,
Now it was a grid of squares lined in tan
A voice said to me, in summer language: Dottie, you are blessed
And I felt the yellow light of the sun eating my face

Then coming upon, a tiny yellow light
So that my face was cored out
In layers of orange-red, then red
You know, it was then, that I had finished something
That the people would like

And faceless, I went in the car, pronounced:
"The book will be called Rome"
Men in the seats
Thinking I was odd or silly
But I could still break them in half

Now it's winter, so I do
If they're lucky
These men I marry
Creaming upon the edge of the nightstand
Little jewels what have you

"These are the things I had been waiting for,"
I answered haughtily, that July
To the sky
To no one

IT IS QUIET

It is quiet when we go
And no no
Nothing is anything if you say that it is
It is quiet and not a sound
But before that: the music
And the hats with their off colors
Marching down the road in a line
In a line of things
Away from us

FEBRUARY 21ST

It is February 21, 2013
My friend has just sent me a poem about traveling
It will never be 2/21/2010 again
I will go back and forth and never be
As if it weren't my task to notice but it is
The blue trees
As if it weren't my task to be here but it is

Out the window there is a man who stares at me
From the trees

Is it true that all trees are the same
All houses are the same
Is it true that all people are the same
We eat from the same china
And the sound is similar
A very similar sound

I would never for example
Leave someone waiting
In the cold for hours
Again
As I have done this man

Outside my window
In the trees

They say he waits for me
But I am confused
As to what that might mean
They say he waits
But I wait too
They say he goes
But I go too
Endless suffering and circle
Long stem palm tree
In the centerpiece

February 21st is a hard day for me
It is also Eric Baus' birthday
Eric Baus is my best friend
There I said it again

He very rarely sends me new poems
But when he does
I smile and nod
And am as tiny as a sail
What Eric Baus is to me
Is white snow
Is forest tree before the beginning

No one wants to compare life to a tumor
Because to think about a tumor is to go out
To think about disease is to go out
No one wants to go out
They want to fly as a burning bird through the sky
They want to forget about it

The state of engaging with this
With a tumor
With that thing that is leaving me
The state of engaging with the leaving
Is to be shy
And I don't know
I don't want to be shy anymore

No I want to sing
And never stop
And never stop listening
To my friends
Who easily could seem as a group
That is everchanging
But is never changing
Are the same people
I know

And not the people in the world
But in the next

And when I thought about
My friend the traveler
No, I have known him
I was right

And when a new person said
He knew me in another life and
I thought no
I was right
Because what is knowing
No
Because I don't know anyone
And I don't owe anything
To anyone
Anymore

Except my self
Which they asked for
When they gave me this life
To go and circle
The endless trees
They gave me the soft brush to contend with
The camera spinning to shoot with
They gave that yellow
Purse to carry
With dead bugs in it
And I had to carry it

All the way through
The trees
And back up to the house again

And when I said I couldn't believe that you came back
I really meant to say
This again
Or we know what this is for
I meant to say
Here we go again
Go through this thing
I meant to say
Thank you for before
When you did all that for me
And I just silently knew
And took your coat off

And anyway
I guess I won't go to sleep
I guess I will wear a ring upon my finger
And won't take it off
And it will be lapis
And I will wear it and wear it
And then have no fingers at all

And if you think I am not hungry
If you think I am not hungry anymore

You are wrong

I am very much so
I very much want to eat the thing
If you think I am not hungry anymore
Then you are very wrong

And I will eat and eat
And consume you
If you think I won't consume you friend
You are wrong

It is 2/21
And so I must go
I must be
With this time
Which is yours and mine
Which is not
I must be in the time
That is all of us

And what is not
Well I'll never know
I will quench the thirst of my stomach
And eat the bitter doughnuts
Under the blank sky
Which we have paid for

And what it was
And what it is
It is again

THE EMPTY COLISEUM

In the center of it all, there is an empty circle

Where thousands of years ago the people the animals fought

No it is only the hay where before

They brought the sheep in

No before the sheep they made the hay

And forgot about it

I am no more a warrior on the sun

I make words

And I made them for a very long time with acquaintances

I hated most of all when they talked about feelings

It was a long time if they felt me, if ever

So I took the I as bloody as it came

And put it on the platter for them to eat

Now I am greying

In the middle of my own and personal library

What to do, was it all a menagerie

Even when I can speak no longer

I will make in full the anonymous I

Or I will make you in full in the anonymous I

I will fill the poems with great pain

And then suck out the meat so that they are only

Shells with only the memory of meat

So that they are only the memory of blood

So I will spill my own so as to make a fresh memory

They said the clouds remember nothing

But in the open arena

There are only real clouds

Not the memory of people

Who are looking

LILAC

I felt empty
As I always had
Because in my past life
I had burned to death

Because in this one
You told me I was a bad poet
As if I cared about poetry
At all

As if I didn't only care
About the little dog
In her bed
Sleeping for all eternity next to me

Lilacs bloom
From the edge of the wood
I walk the grass-lined streets
To come to a lemon tree

What a blank and edible flower
The lilac is
It is as if your face
Were there inside of me

Or on that tree
White-lined
And inside your heart
A glowing purple, a glowing green

It is as if I had made you believe
In me once again
It is as if you knew I was your true love
It was as if I didn't have to know

In this life
All you were to me
Was that flower

I KNOW THERE IS ANOTHER WORLD

I know there is another world
And the people with their round heads
I know there is a sunset made of sand
I know they count in fours just to listen to me
They like the click click click, click
I know the people listen to me
On the other side
That's why I get the root from the left side of the dresser
And put it in the inky water
I drink the tea with the elephants under a taboo shelter
To sip with our trunks
Not really space
To say I was not really space at all
Going and going
I always said
I was the poem thing
I always knew the people in the other world
I always knew my spirit husband
Waited for me
Under the palm trees
I know he still waits for me
His blue-green arms outstretched
I know he sings for me a lullaby
That only we know

I know I have had other children
And they sit in blocks of ice
On another planet
Waiting for me to leave this world
And take the rainbow flame to them
To give them my hand and voice
To give them my head again
To give them my lips and eyes
To give them my beak
All done here for all the taking
To give them my body
I know my children and husband wait for me
In the other world
To give myself over once again

A NEW REALITY

I am in the hills of Europe
No the banks of the Tiber

Everything is beautiful
But it is not you

Women wear so much person
Red and white and yellow and white

But to think I will never smell your hair in the rain
Is something I cannot bear

All the facts and figures
All the mathematics of an entire generation

All the mathematics in ten layers of being
Will never equal my love for you

Will never equal what it means to have lost you
Dear She-wolf, my She-wolf, to not have you here with me

LILAC FIELD

To perform death is something only humans would do
No animal would sit there
With a blank look on its face
Just because the camera is there

No no an animal would look directly in it
Or cover its face, like the overweight
Woman in the picture in the magazine
By the room where I keep my bed

What people don't understand about beauty
Is that after all it is not fleeting
After all it is so gross to be that way
That someone sees among you

After all, to call into question
I painted my lips, my eyes
Only our scholars know that
To perform is to be malleable

To perform in language
Or was it
The large purple insect I let in the room
Or was it the furred face—the hippo or the gorge

That I was the devil in the wood
In my own bones that I knew the face
That I took that face
Was it midnight blue sky

No, were my wings iridescent
Even in these lines
The voice moves you
What sense of exquisite cause

Thought
Moves you past these lines
Into conversation
With the undead

I don't know
That is something
You will have to answer for yourself
I came back to this place to help you

And that I did
Shoot sparks of green and grey
Through time
What skin sack

I put myself in
I mean for what, why,
Or who
Did I manage to do this for if not you

Lilaced thing
The soft rustle of beetle wings
In air that is warm and grey
And is not strong

But there is there to carry us past it

THE GROVELER

You want me to abject myself
And tell you how grateful I am that you talked to me
I am grateful I am grateful
Thank you for talking to me
I am at your feet
Ready to do the walking for you
Your words move through my mouth
I am ready to speak for you
And I will do so
You were
Something or someone I loved
But I am a traveler
And I love no one
But the empty road
That guides me to the next person
That shows me only to my maker
That says eat eat when it finds the lonely hunter
I don't know I had an axe but I did not cut you down
Got you a hundred presents
And fed you and brought you a violet wrap
And wrapped you in tinfoil
Sweet sweet little candied fish
I would have liked to taste the sugar off your skin
Instead now I realize the rotting from within

The sugar the ice on planets and stars
The romance of the evening
Coated in ice from your dead flesh
Already rotting from within

MOVING

Yes, I am moving but I am not
I will never see my body dead
In the way I have seen yours

The soul never sleeps
I told you
After you were gone

What was your name
I kept moving on
Until I did not need you anymore

I kept entering the same day
Until it was not the same day
Anymore, I left it

I thought of one universal thought
The idea that we all feel
The same way

But it was a new kind of water
I was swimming in
It was a new place

I was going to

THE BED

I don't even sleep in my bed anymore
I just go and sleep in the room
With the old woman who understands me
She waited on this earth for me
She didn't die for me
We sleep and sleep
And we are in love

I don't sleep with men anymore
In any way
There I said it, in this poem
I say it all of the time to the people around
I tell the people around
No I don't belong to anyone
Because I don't and I never did and that's the truth

If I belong to anything it is to the Prince of Wands
On a chariot of burning ash I see him coming towards me
Or waiting there
Should I go to him
His skin is clear and young
But his eyes are old old
Or they are not, but they are deepening so fast

Deepening so fast that they blacken and twist
He has four virgins to his side
He has a lion with which he travels
He has a box of things that are separate and strange
I think when he looks this way and that
That he is making a play for me
I think in so many ways he does it all for me

What would it be like
To leave and go
To leave and go
Most do nothing
What would it be like: I touch the sun
And it doesn't even care
It expects me

I have lived this life with some relationship to the moon
But the sun has glowed and burst
Seeing me on a stack of shirts
Sleeping, then not sleeping
Dreaming of burning princes
Waiting for it really
My ferocious, feline suitor

Glistening with yellow charge
Why it has known I would not even be

Part of this
And it didn't wait
But turned in a vortex of time
Until I met up with my friends
And sang a song that it could hear

Blooming sun, it sets a yellow table
With marigolds and ivory shanks
And sits the prince upon it, who has golden threads
In his beard and eyes
And who is not wise, but is a visionary
So that he sees me and you
He can see everything

The Sunday tablecloth
Large and suspect
Yellowing colors, but with orange slices
The prince's eyes
Now yellow too
And on the plates a yellow egg
And lemon

And was it he
Who sang to me
When I was a girl
In the fields of violets

Was it he
Who lifted
The curtain of dawn

To set upon the stage
A clearing of blue
And in the distance the forest of wonder
The stag, silver and sure of himself
Who had waited
For this moment
Throughout a lifetime

Who is to know
I sleep and sleep
And the old woman wakes me
She knows it is another day
And we whistle while we go about
Feeding the children and opening the house
To the other people

In the midst of this
I take her up
Just breeze her up
Into my arms
And when we kiss I know it was worth everything
And when I kiss my one true love
It is true, I know

I know I know
I will never truly be a person
I am a devil
No, a demon
A red-heather belly
The red-lace of eyes
Or a shoot of green

Always coming from something
I was never here
I was never there
You thought I was
You thought
You'd seen the last of me
But I will never die

And you will
And you will die
No you will die
And when you ask for my mercy
It won't be I
But she
Who will give it to you

And merciful she is
Or so it seems
But the sad truth is

On this earth
And the next
There is some such thing
As patience
But no such thing
As mercy

No no
No such thing
As mercy

ONCE IT'S IN THE PICTURE

Once climax is in the picture
The desire is over
But baby I desire you over and over
And it never stops
And when I really get going
I really get going
You animal lover
Your face has stripes and eyes
Just like the devil
But you are even worse than that
You don't even move
Just a tiny lump of flesh
I animate over and over
A doll with bright blond hair
I rock back and forth
In my chair with my babies
With my little fowl and kin
With green flowers
That flowers
And flowers
And flowers and flowers

POEM TO FLORENCE

It took a year without you
To make me write about you
Strange California city on the peninsula
I could have sworn
Had I been there before

My lover who said I connected him to his forgotten things
What is the dull river Lethe
I don't know, but I think it's evil
And when I drink of it I don't see stars
Instead I see the lime groves

I see a dull aching fall
With limes and peaches
I see a woman
I could have sworn
That I'd seen her before

Grass green fence
It is there
So we hop along it
Until the place of fawns and simple things
The pink azaleas blooming in the shaded wood

A child I'd seen there before
Who could have—was she mine
No no but she was my sister
My sister with her mouth so heavy
So full of things she'd wished she'd said

There were things I wished I'd said
And done
But it is too late now
So I go
Heavy with my offering
This book, this book

I WANT TO BE ALIVE

More than anything I want to be alive
I want to jiggle
I want to jiggle on you
And gurgle
And urinate on your backspan
I want you to eat my menstrual blood
And soft juices
I want to eat your shit until I dream
I want you to come shit all over me
I want to bury my vomit in your shit
I want you to kiss me hard hard
In the nighttime
And not give up
I don't want to be a thing
I want to be becoming
The nighttime
I want to be the nighttime with you
You know, I loved you
I loved you
I was wrong

THE DOGS

The dogs run away
And around the streets

I see their bodies and want them immensely

To be with me until the end
I can imagine a hundred of them

All by my bedclothes
Waiting to be fed

I think I like the animal
Because it doesn't give up much of a fuss

I hate the people who depend on me to live
But an animal who does it is of the other place

You are the kind of thing who takes from me
And never gives anything away

And when you call to me with your synchronicity
I can't help but run to you

You my horrible star
I can't help but run to you when you call for me

YOU THINK LANGUAGE IS SILLY UNTIL IT HAPPENS TO YOU

I write you
From above an ocean

Wilted and stale flower
I used to think you were odd

Until you burst in my mouth
Like the most obvious thing

All in all I was glad I had had
Another moment in the rain with you

What is all this beauty
If you can't cast a thing beside it

It was me, I astounded everything
Even the animals almost gone in the basin

You walking towards me
In the ghostly smoke

When you took off your raincoat
It was not to keep you hungry

It was not to keep you simple
It was to keep you wet

Wet and violent flower
That I shook at the people

When I described you as an ocean
It was because I was still close to it

When I looked on you dead center
It was to remember the thing with the soft outlines

It was to remember the thing
I had grown used to forgetting

COMPLAINERS

Some people don't want to die
Because you can't complain when you're dead
I hope heaven is just a bunch of men lying around
Ready to do what I say
Ready with dicks and some such
When I'm dead I won't be looking for a partner
As much as a heavenly creature
After all I was promised virgins
But I don't care about that as much
As the eyes looking into me in abandon
Like porn but better
Because there will be no screen
There will be no holy divider then
Between me and my brethren
And the smell of sunshine
Will emit from every brow
That's the kind of thing I expect from death
That's the kind of thing I'm waiting for

SADNESS

I feel
Actually beside myself

Like beside my self
Like be side my self
Like really

Recall the sense of self
The lemon air in deep summer
Recall the look

The look that meant nothing
Recall the nothing
That you meant to me

You with your brown hair
Nothing worse
Than a head full of brown hair

What could be worse
Than a head
Full of brown hair

I'd rather be hairless
Than to see your hair
All loose and dark and shiny

WHY IS A MOUSE SAD?

Why are mice so sad, with their crying faces
And why do they perform a shard of sadness in me
To see them
To create a mood of their scurrying
I don't know I don't know
I feel safe without them
With them, it is all horrible
Like anything could happen

Did you know that the universe
Unfolds a million times below and beneath
The scale that we exist in?
More than a million
This knowledge is astounding
It makes me realize
Just how dumb I am
And how silly we are to be afraid

Here are mice on our scale
And the universe below and beneath
And above
And airplanes
And places that scale the sky

Are just animals within the animals
And being a human is nothing
It is a construct we have created

Disregarding constructs, I want to murder all mice
I want to murder them and snuff out their sadness
And I want to flip their bodies in the air
And prevent them from enduring
An eternal sadness of being laid out
As human corpses
And the eternal sadness
Of body becoming word

What word might I transfer to a mouse
To let them know how I feel
Nothing. What words can I say to the nanoscale
To make it hear me? Nothing. It will be silence
What words can I say to the dark macrocosm
That is circling above me? Nothing.
I am dizzy. I am dizzy in its magnitude
My body is so small, it might as well not even exist, at all

In face of it all, I speak softly
In face of everything I write loud words
I color the pages of the book
Which is actually the wall
I get frightened by the shudder of the bodies next to me

Who are ghosts
Who I love despite the fact
I will never understand them

Nor will they ever understand me
Bright lights circling in some other macrocosm
Loved ones, who are ghosts, loved ones
My loved ones swirling above me
And I am so alone
And I am alone here
With the idea of ghosts
And the idea of humanity, which is a cruel idea

Humanity is a cruel idea but not a sad one
Animal ideas are sad, but only because they
Are the same as me, and I can't ever admit it
And to have a soft patch of eye and bone
Is a kind of sadness you will never get over
And to have a voice is to not have it one day, too
Which is awful
Which is much worse than to never have a body again

I think instead of being sad
At death
I'll sleep with mice
And have them crawl on my legs and hands
And I will open my eyes for them to put their eyes upon

And I will open my mouth
So that they can crawl in
And make their nest

What flattening it would be to be a mouse home
To take in the sadness
And thus negate it
And to cancel out humanity
By them inside of me
And I wouldn't let anyone kill them
If they resided within me
Not even me. I wouldn't even let myself kill them

And you
I wouldn't let you take them
With your cruel sadness
And I would no longer feel the pressure to be human
And to change my mouse behavior
And to change my behavior
Which is gentle
Which only wants to love and live
And never go away

I FEEL PITY

I feel pity for my sister who is dying somewhere in a lonely
    house
I feel pity for my dog who had to die without me on a table
    after months of pain
I feel pity for the stranger in the hospital bed who is never
    touched but sleeps there nonetheless
What love for me
What love for them I feel
Absolute pity, tenderness
I feel pity and sadness for the children in the schools who are
    not given a fair shot
I feel pity for the books that are published and then burned
With bodies that fell a thousand trees
I feel pity for the trees
Left outside in the cold and wind
To fend for themselves with roots so thick, and no one sees
I feel pity for the sky, with blue vapors
It hugs the clouds, and the clouds don't care
I feel pity for my legs, this desk
I feel pity for this desk, its wooden face
Won't I just throw it away when I am done with it
I feel pity for the moon
Raging against the day, and what for, its crazy face
All ghostly, that is what they really say about it

I feel pity for the stars, the blue stars, and the red stars
And the green stars, I feel pity for the stars that shoot sparks
And the green-grey
I feel pity for the colors
I feel pity for this room
Where I will go and bring a life in
I feel pity for that life, and more
I feel pity for all of the lives
That go on and no one even stops to notice
I feel pity for the flowers
The birds, all of them
And even pity for the birds
But I don't feel pity for you
I don't pity you
You big hot thing
I don't feel pity for your arms
Which could hold for me a thousand hours
And I want them to
I don't feel pity for you
Among all these things, I love you more
More and most of all
And you are careless, and ceaseless
Like you always are to everyone
I don't feel pity
You have this poem, this book
I don't feel pity
They will talk of you for a thousand years

You gorgeous spirit you
You crazy nothing
Blond hair and sublime torso
Smile more than a million men
A truly million dollar man
In greenish suit
Wild spirit, you
I love you
I love you when you're rocking
I love you when you're rocking
Always for me
But never for me
Always always
In the wind

GEORG TRAKL IN THE GREEN SUN

Georg Trakl, in the sun
I am in love with you
I want you to come back to this earth
So that we can be lovers
I will wash your hallucinatory sheets
With bleach
And give birth to your Austrian kin
It took a while
Now I am me
You were always you
Come back to this earth
I will wash you in a bath of violet milk
I will take all of your cares away
I will be your mother father
I will be your sister, little bunny
I will birth you in the ocean
And when your head disconnects from your body
I will scoop up the black water
Until I find it
And put it in a pail of blue
And sail the ocean back to land
To put your eyelids in a jar
A tiny capsule
To take with me, everything

Yes I will eat

I will swallow your eyelashes

And if you don't think I'm serious

And if you don't think I am serious this time, poetry

I am

TO DREAM

I was living
But to wake into the dream
To sleep and not sleep
And to not make
Anything
But a world that was always a dream
So that I never knew what it was to be alive

What is living
But fear
Orange couch and drink with bitters
Water too and leavened animal
Or what the world wants
My eyes do not make
Whatever color they are

Still, song and breath are there in dreams, too
And people coming to your aid
And when I was sorry in my dream
It was part of this one
That I felt such remorse
For things I did not know
Or could not

And green cockatoo that landed in a hazy nightmare
Were its eyes sullen or surprised
When I took my hand from behind the bed
And held the pickaxe
Sliced him in half
And soldered to one half part of a man
And to the other, my soul, which was dead by then
And an offering

WILD

It's like the world went wild
Wild with me
And I couldn't stop it anymore
I was a really good poet
But more than that
I wanted you to not have to
Eat the pigs with the other ones
Baby honey baby
When I think of your head and breastbone
I go wild
You wear the red necklace
And I sweat sweat on the pavement
Still I think I will take the crushing pain
To whatever narrative
The men talk of
Whatever thing they mean
Means fire
I think I will wake and walk
And walk with you
Until they put me under
Until they put me under
I will cross the blue forest
With only you on my mind
Dumb spirit

Only you on my mind

You made me dumb

When I had only you on my mind

So I took the red necklace

Dumb spirit

There there

Always always always always

Always always always

Always on my mind

WHAT IS A MAN IF NOT A SIPHON

Don't talk to me about class
A man writes a bourgeois poem and you don't even care about it

But to me you give me a letter
Call me a thing that a million others deserved

I have come to terms with who I am
But who are you and have you

I don't have time but have one arm closed tightly on the tree
    that is outside of the song
My friend wants to go into his bed and be in the song but it is
    lonely for him

My fear extends into the stars
Don't you know I never will

I will go to Paris and then to the exaltation
Remember only the poems that gave me a fair shake

You took my poems and threw them in the air
But these are not air poems

These are, or what are they
Oh what are they

I have to go to the post office
No I have to go to the dead

One arm so tightly on the tree outside of it
I would I could start to think that I don't care about the song
    after all

And would you care
When everyone lies so furiously, so ferociously they tell lies
    within the winter

I went there with my hair in my hands
And he didn't take it for a sixth time

But by then my hands were both so tightly on the tree
I told myself I didn't care about the song

His lips and head were boring
And I was sick of his smell

I wrapped myself in leaden sheets
And sank deep into my own infernal ocean

And there I was
Until you picked this poem up, so hello, hello there

You sickly thing
It is these words now that are your medicine

DAWN SONG

When I hear sweet songs I think of you
I don't know why, but I do
When I hear sweet songs I think of you

You don't believe me
But it's true
When I hear sweet songs I think of you

You went along
You thought I knew
When I hear sweet songs I think of you

But I am dumb
I never knew
So I wandered thru and thru

Dear thing of mine
When I hear sweet songs
I think of you

You don't believe me
But it's true
When I hear sweet songs I think of you

POEM FOR MY FRIEND

Is it possible that it is grief that brought us together
Yes it is
It is possible

Dear friend, we sat on the sun-soaked fields
But I would have a strawberry with you anywhere
Or when they said of Julius Caesar: that his life was gentle

Dear friend, I would paint your eyes anywhere
The elements so mixed up in me
That Nature might stand up and say: Now this is a man!

And when they burn me up into the trees
I hope you are the trees
The set of neat green things

Come waiting for me
I hope you are the bushes
I hope you are the neat green bushes

There waiting for me

RELATIVE CERTAINTY

I am relatively certain that I was an animal in a past life
Why do I know
Because of my snout
Because of the fur that surrounds me
Because of my love
My She-wolf my She-wolf
I love you

All of my hormones
The naked body
And then the dead one
The days, sweet and long
And then no dates at all
Utter space
To make a deal with

I am relatively certain
It was the fur that was important
Before I was trapped in this body
I know before the planets engulfed me
I looked at people and tried to talk
And it was my vocabulary, my tone
That did me in

THE STATIC NATURE OF IT ALL

I wake up in a house full of trash
And eat some cheese before I go out in the heat
Everything just doesn't move
When you can't make it to
Another day, another let me think about this
But you don't call you don't write you don't care
You don't want to see me
I want to see you so bad
But what is the trees that give shade
Even in my own voice I am calming
But what are the glowing yellow bunnies I kick around
You know what is going on
Still you stand there stand there
Even though I am the one from the other world
Who is in love with you
It's hard for me to even defend you
To the legions of seers, crazy birds and bugs
That I call my "friends"
Even as they try to mix the potions for me
They can't help but ask me why why
Why this one
And it's hard for me to say anything
When you just sit there every day, so still and boring

Just the static nature of it

And I go looking looking for you in the streets

And I never find you

I never find you at all

PALM TREE

The last kiss I will ever take
Will not be with you
But with my child
I will feel the breath leaving me
I will feel not the endless circle but the broken one

And the green tongue they will place on my lips
Will be soft like breezes
Pillows and the orange flowers

I remember when I was born
Everything seemed really new
I was blue
Then I woke up and I belonged again
To someone

THE WALL HANGING I NEVER NOTICED

I never noticed before
How the red flowers hang from the blue branches
I never noticed before the light in this room
I never noticed the way the air is cool again
I never noticed anything but you
But you but you
So that I couldn't sleep
I never noticed what was anything but you
Until I noticed you
And could not help it
Until I noticed you I could not help it
Until you made the red flowers alive again
Until the blue branches
The lemons you loved, but also the way you loved me, too
Until all of this I never noticed you
But once I did
I never minded noticing
I never stopped noticing
Until I noticed you
I never stopped noticing
Until you, I never stopped

THE RAIN

What is going to happen
Is that it's going to rain

Rain my love
A poem not about sex

But love
The true kind

You talk of things
To myself and others

You think of things
Her long tanned arms

You will realize you love me
But it will be too late

You will cry out for me
I will be long gone

This is not a wish
But what I knew to be so

This is what I knew to be so
Under the pouring sun

This is what I knew to be so
Under the pouring sea

Where they will find us
You and me

THE ART DECO OF THE WEST

In every scene I am a young woman

In every scene I am a young girl
Waiting to be helped by the train conductor

The silent geometry of the sun

In every scene I am waiting for you
To be with me in dreams

To hold my beige suitcase, as we wander out the door

On the train to the West
They have very old people

Who do not need my help
But help me

Move my brightly colored cases
Into the waiting room

In the night, every night that there is
I call out for you

Is it Tuesday, Saturday
Months go by

I am no longer a girl
Nor was I when we met

You were a boy
I forget about that

I forget that you still are
I look at the faces of men

And they have more grit than you
Still you are so beautiful to me

Did I ever tell you
Did I ever tell you

The orange sun
Did I ever tell you sun that I and only I love you

Did I ever tell you I lied
I lied

I lied
I said I was here before

I never was here
I walked along with my suitcase alone

Then I slept in a bed of ocean colors
And you did not care

You turned dead snakes in your bed
The snakes that were red, and gold, and green

And forgot about me
You forgot about me

And what I meant to you
And then it was over

And this was Rome
A placid town on the sea

And this was the place we lived together
Where I said I love you I love you I love you

Over and over
Until I couldn't speak anymore

SONNET WEATHER

I daresay it is sonnet weather
And may be 12–16 lines long of sun
I have disillusionment of all o'clocks
After all all I wanted was to be hairless
But you wanted me full of hair
And then nothing
The hair weights down
It makes a mat
I tell you it gets wet and makes a furry mat
Like a face
Except a face has bone and skin too
But a hair just has a hair
Oh I think it is hair weather
Out and out I forget I am dying

I AM A CORPSE

I am a corpse
And you are a corpse
And in the nighttime
I see your arm on me and it is dead already
And my arm is dead already
And I look at my belly, already blue
And it is barren and empty
And my lack of pain is also a kind of death
And I drift off to sleep and then I wake
And it is all dying
Why? Because a demon is after me
And he she it has been
Since the day I was born
What an unrepentant ass I must have been
In my past lives
Or what a soulless fish I must have fished
In this one
I can feel the endless stream of words
That are not flesh
They might as well be
Dreams and too
It is the work of corpses
Not ghosts
Come on all you corpses

Just dance and fuck

I just don't want to animate

This rancid flesh

Like you do

Anymore

So I will say goodbye

And say

Fuck you

And I love you

And I never did

I never knew what feeling was

I only felt the pain

The sun the moon the trees the stars

The animals the birds the words

I only felt the pain

The things the you inflicted on me

THERE ARE A MILLION YOUNG MEN

And that reality
It's like fuck fuck get me away from all of this
There is hair and men and hair to greedy my grubby
Hands on
The reality
That not one of them is special
Or that not one of them can be let in this castle
Or that not one of them is available in the night to converse
But my lonely lonely slipper
I put it on and go dancing
But only in my head
And say, slipper, my slipper
I adorned you with rubies
And then, just look at you
The red reflecting in winter seascape
Nothing could be more important
Nothing could take my breath away
Faster
Than that

IF I THOUGHT OF ANYTHING

If I thought of anything of this fall
It was the cold and the neverending sickness
It was the calls again and again
Not from friends
But only people who wanted something from me
Not even something very good
I had nothing to offer
I gave my love freely to the children and to the people
Who were so blissfully important to the edges of the fire
I could not lose them, even when I tried to
If I could think of this fall, there is the thought of orange
When Will said the trees looked as if the brush had brushed
   them so
I thought of what it meant to brush them so
The magic of the evening, in the cold
A half-hearted attempt not to be dead
But no no
No now I have a purpose
And you can all laugh at me all that you want to
But I know I'm right
Always have been
I was actually born into this
A long lineage of things you can't even begin to fathom
I'm sorry, but it's true

And you may be or not
Right
That's not really the purpose or the point of it
I went in and out
We don't own anything
The flesh is very silly
Consciousness is actually a flash in the pan
If you think this is not my green face flashing
In a whole shower of electricity
Over your face and spirit sitting there
Then I don't know what else to offer you
But the drab grey morning and night
When I was there, in the midst of the other morning
The purple light
When I saw the sunshine and his smile
Hey, I know he's kissed a million women
Oh and even though he will always forget me
I will wait for him
I will wait for him, you silly people
Because even with that unknowing expression
That one, that one
That one is the one that I love
He found me, you see
I didn't look for him
He found me
In the poem and then he was there
And the years and years will pass

It is the one I love

Time doesn't matter, I told you

And when you see him

You had better throw your hats down

That's the face that made them all leave the city

And fight

That's the face

We talk about in whispers

But oh no, it's not his face

It's the heart the heart

THE DEAD OWE A LOT OF TAXES

My dead relatives owe a lot of taxes
So I eat some chocolate wafers and think about it
Not you, because you love are dead
Just a bunch of cutesy nothing
Am I the only one who notices this
It would be easier if you didn't like women
But I know what Greek Art is
And I once made a sculpture
The sad thing is people give me advice
Really at the helm I will always do the wrong thing
God I just thought you were someone
Now the witch tells me it's just the blue sign in the doorway
So I shut my eyes until the world drops dead
So I shut my eyes and hope that you might be replaced
But really I will have to work
This is the dark night of the soul
And I am so wild baby
But not for you anymore
Which is so sad for you
Oh even you can realize just how sad that is

THE END

Promising myself I would not do this again
Is what kept me going

A friend told me to
And I listened

Taking a thing to the end of its life
Is what I was made to do

I think I am not attuned
To the things that breathe

Well that's not true
I am in tune to breath and life

And little falls of flowers

When the moon was high
I went out to the stream

And brought in the water
For my folks, my kin, my brethren

I brought in the greenish milk
To feed the ones who were already dying

Oh did they go
Oh I do not know

THERE IS NOTHING

I remember how he looked when I ran to meet him
I remember sitting with our heads touching and the night trees
I remember how I went and walked
It meant nothing
It means nothing
There is nothing
But this
But this

ROME

I

I always loved you
And I didn't love him
And I used you
As a counterpoint to what I didn't like
But you weren't you
That I loved you
And didn't love him
Was some sort of thing
That wasn't true

II

In time spent with you
I always laughed
A million hours
Of moods and emotions
Or that I perceived it so
But really that young guy
Who cared about emotions
Is dead
And in his place a bitter man
Growing fat and embittered
And more or less that potential
Over and over again
Your calcified heart
That I said I'd put up with
If only I could talk to
Your calcified cock
But really it was your dead heart
That would have done us in

III

Rome is about the Colosseum
Said the cashier in the local market
Where I went with my mother
In the town I grew up in
No longer a young man
But tunneling towards a ferocity
Not anyone could have predicted
When my soft smile
Smiled at those who
Only looked at me
But now I look
At the cashier
Straight in the eye
As he said in Rome
It was all about governments
Ruled by Cardinals
But instead of clergymen
I thought of red birds
My father and I used to stare at
Through the window of our yellow house
So many years ago

IV

I guess I had to go to the woods
It was part of this pilgrimage
To get rejected so vehemently
Over and over again
Until some said it was the rejection I was after
No it wasn't
I wanted the intensity that you sometimes promised
You made the illusory moon in the doorway
You wanted me to stare at the ceiling
How else to
I believed it was that young heart
That I fell in love with
Not the bitter one
And as we grow older my love
You know it just gets older and older
And mine just gets younger
Wilder
My heart more an animal
You know my love
You are already dead
And you were when I met you at the Guggenheim
And later when you squealed at the fast cab
Even though I should have been turned off
Maybe it was your weakness that made me think
You weren't already dead

But you are
You died that first year in the cold
Just like the people told me
So boring to think of
Not Art Deco not the West
But as boring to talk about as the weather channel
As boring to hear about as the men discussing golf

V

In Baltimore the towns are so close to the capitol
That when I went there with my friends to see
Poets like the hot Adam Robinson
I felt like, oh this is Rome
Like when I hid in the midst of it
I said I could stare at the ceiling in the dark
In my warm bed
But a person can make a beautiful bed
And murder you in it
And that's what you did
And not fuck me in it
I want to be clear
About this bodily rejection
That you rejected my body so strongly
That my poems about corpses will always be about you
You told me I was safe
And then you murdered
Women everywhere
The ones you don't care about
Still the sister
And I want you
The truth of it
Me wanting you
In dead linens
Maybe to swaddle you

And that is what we do with a lover
And no you're not that
That you made sure
Maybe to hold my eye to yours
So you can really see what you have given up
So you can truly see what you have given up
When at sixty it might hit you
What you have given up
When your sentimental heart
Might let its hair down and see
The sun for the first time

VI

I remember the irony you said

That it was this person

This person in the poem

That first attracted me to you

That this I is what might connect me to you

It turned me on you

You silly little girl

We are in the dirty dirty forum

And I have my swords

And you are so shored up

Are you even defenseless

No you have your back to me

Rushing off to your home

And I am turning and turning for the crowd

Have my dead tigers twisting for me

Playing dead

My metal dress

Perverse obsessions

And it is only now

That I realize I am bleeding

Now no air now dead

And that it was your careful strike

That made it so

VII

Just a few days ago
I cried in a purple frock
Ready to meet my friend
At the French restaurant
So tired I cried
Not to my friend
But to myself in the mirror
And I said get it together, Dottie
And then later a week later
Adam said the night cools
Then he said grow up
Now I cry against glass
That only shows myself
And say I will kill you
A sexless tiger
I will say what is your life
If not no one wants you
Only to track blood across cold snow
So I said no I will kill the next competitor
No I said I will hold my hand out again
When I meet him in the coliseum ground

VIII

We both know
That the moon isn't you
Or the him isn't you
We both know you aren't you
You know you aren't you
You are a patrician in a nice house
Going home to your family house
We both know you will never be
Banned from the city to the countryside
We both know you are another rich bourgeois boy
With little talent who will do something simple
We both know that you are a simple guy
Who saw the savagery of my body
And pushed it away like an old serving maid
Disposable
Forgetting even though you shouldn't have
What I could do to you
Even you forgot that this sort of thing was possible
And that you should be careful
You weren't careful
Because part of you believed every lie I told you
Because most of you is dead
And the parts that aren't
Will soon be

IX

Sometimes I forget I am dead already
Love I am dead now said my friend
Sometimes I forget the emptiness of the arena
That this page is what I carve into
And that everyone has gone home to their families
And that I feast on air
My own dead desire
That always wins as it loses
Augustus and Livy
And the battle of Zama and the battle of Alesia
The curved blade
The coin with my face on it
The man you were in 50 BC
Who picked up the coin with my face on it
Who put it in your pocket to give to a sweetheart
Until moments later another part of me
Came rushing up and killed you
Just because you dared get in here
In empty places
My empty heart
Where only a dumb coward
Would wander in
On the way to the marketplace

X

Under the arena they keep the animals

Ready to be killed

But don't get excited

These animals aren't you

Red tiger black lion white macaque blue macaw

With blue eyes

The fortune of admiration

Don't get too excited

You aren't an animal

But a man who killed me

Now I am in a dirty arena

With no other human

The sun has snow on it

They bring up cats, bears, a rodent

And I kill them all

Even the two-headed beast with the snake for tail

And fanned crown

Is dead

It's easy to kill

They bring up my own dead body

Propped over with dead desire

And I kill it

They bring up my daughter

Her wolf eyes

A sign of recognition and with my hand on her neck

I say goodbye
Never bringing you up
You already went home five years ago
And sleep so quietly and soundly
With your family and frankincense
And your Christianity and Christmases
And bursting silver buckles
This isn't about you
This was and has always been about
The real
Bloody and awful
Twisting and twisting
Love is a strange dance
I do with myself
But I won't give it up
Renting a car two thousand years later
To go driving the dark streets
Full of ghosts
Classic nitrogen and the dogs in the distance
One of those ghosts I know, lover
Will be you
And when I find that ghost
Only you know
Only we know
What we will do with it

ACKNOWLEDGMENTS

Thank you to the following editors of the following publications who included poems from this book in earlier forms: *Academy of American Poets*; *American Poetry Review*; *BODY*; *Boston Review*; *Clinic Presents*; *Forklift, Ohio*; *Granta*; *Gulf Coast*; *Harvard Advocate*; *Mead: The Magazine of Literature and Libations*; *Phantom Limb*; *Poetry*; *Poetry Northwest*; *Paris Review*; and *Tin House*. Thank you to Black Ocean for including "Depression" in their *Private Policy!* anthology and thank you to Literary House Press for including the poem "You think language is silly until it happens to you" in their *The Book of Scented Things: An Anthology of Contemporary American Poetry*.

ABOUT THE AUTHOR

Dorothea Lasky is the author of *Thunderbird*, *Black Life*, and *AWE*, and is also the coeditor of *Open the Door: How to Excite Young People About Poetry*. She is an assistant professor of poetry at Columbia University's School of the Arts and lives in Brooklyn.